W9-ASN-949

W. K. Kellogg

History Maker Bios

Laura Hamilton Waxman

LERNER PUBLICATIONS COMPANY • MINNEAPOLIS

For Caleb, a lover of cereal and all manner of carbohydrates.

Text copyright © 2007 by Laura Hamilton Waxman
Illustrations copyright © 2007 by Lerner Publications Company

Illustrations by Big Time Attic

Lerner Publications Company
A division of Lerner Publishing Group
241 First Avenue North
Minneapolis, MN 55401 U.S.A.

Website address: www.lernerbooks.com

Library of Congress Cataloging-in-Publication Data

Waxman, Laura Hamilton.
    W. K. Kellogg / by Laura Hamilton Waxman ; illustrations by Big Time Attic.
        p.   cm. —   (History maker bios)
    Includes bibliographical references and index.
    ISBN-13: 978–0–8225–6578–9 (lib. bdg. : alk. paper)
    ISBN-10: 0–8225–6578–1 (lib. bdg. : alk. paper)
    1. Kellogg, W. K. (Will Keith), 1860–1951—Juvenile literature.
2. Industrialists—United States—Biography—Juvenile literature.
3. Philanthropists—United States—Biography—Juvenile literature. 4. Kellogg Company—History—Juvenile literature. 5. Cereal products industry—United States—History—Juvenile literature. 6. W. K. Kellogg Foundation—History—Juvenile literature. I. Title.
HD9056.U45K458 2007
338.7'6647092—dc22 [B]   2006018507

Manufactured in the United States of America
1 2 3 4 5 6 – JR – 12 11 10 09 08 07

TABLE OF CONTENTS

INTRODUCTION — 5

1. NO TIME FOR PLAY — 6

2. WORK, WORK, AND MORE WORK — 14

3. A FLAKY INVENTION — 20

4. KING OF CORN FLAKES — 27

5. HELPING PEOPLE HELP THEMSELVES — 36

TIMELINE — 44

CEREAL, CEREAL, CEREAL — 45

FURTHER READING — 46

WEBSITES — 47

SELECT BIBLIOGRAPHY — 47

INDEX — 48

INTRODUCTION

Have you heard of Kellogg's Corn Flakes or Rice Krispies or Fruit Loops? These cereals are sold by a company W. K. Kellogg started. W. K. and his brother John Harvey invented the first flaked cereal in 1894. Back then, breakfast cereal was a new idea. W. K. set out to change that.

W. K. opened his company in 1906. He was a hard worker and natural business leader. Soon millions of families began to buy and eat his cereal for breakfast.

W. K. became a rich man. He wanted to do something useful. For W. K., that meant helping people in need. In 1930, he opened the W. K. Kellogg Foundation. This group has helped people around the world.

W. K. worked hard all his life. He shared his success with others.

This is his story.

1 No Time for Play

Willie Keith Kellogg was born on April 7, 1860, to a hardworking family. The Kelloggs lived in Battle Creek, Michigan. Their days were filled with work, work, and more work.

In the mornings, Willie worked in the family's gardens. The Kelloggs sold their fruit and vegetables to townspeople.

Willie's father also owned a broom factory. Willie began working there when he was seven years old. He worked in the afternoons and on weekends. His family expected him to buy his own clothes with the money he earned.

During the day, Willie went to school. He was very shy. Still, he did make a few friends. In class, Willie had trouble reading the chalkboard. Some of his teachers thought he was not very smart. It turned out that Willie needed glasses. But he didn't know that then. His mother and father didn't worry too much about his grades. They thought hard work was more important than education.

In the late 1800s, people made brooms of straw or sticks (RIGHT).

Willie loved his horse, Spot. Spot may have looked like this Arabian horse.

Some days, Willie squeezed in a little time for play. He especially loved to be with his horse, Spot. Someone once told him that Spot was an Arabian, a rare kind of horse. That made Willie love the horse even more.

One day, his father decided to sell Spot. The family needed the extra money. Willie missed the horse terribly. He promised himself that someday he would have many Arabian horses.

Willie's parents were strict with their children. But they were also caring. John and Ann often found ways to help friends and neighbors in need. Once, a nearby family needed milk for their children. Willie's parents gave them one of their two cows. Another time, a neighbor didn't have enough money to keep his farm. John and Ann gave him the money he needed.

A Simple and Honest Life

The Kelloggs belonged to a Christian religion called the Seventh-day Adventists. The Adventists believe in living simple, honest lives. They encourage members to do good deeds for others. One of their biggest goals is to help people stay healthy. The Adventists teach people not to smoke or drink alcohol. They also believe in eating healthy foods. As an adult, Kellogg did not belong to any religion. But he followed many of the beliefs he had learned as an Adventist.

By the age of fourteen, Willie had grown into a skinny, serious young man. Around that time, he began to go by the name Will. He quit school. Then Will became a full-time broom salesperson. He used a horse and buggy to travel from town to town. For longer sales trips, Will sometimes took a train. He loved the adventure of this newer and faster kind of travel.

Will stands with some of the brooms he sold.

Will's early business trips on trains began a love of travel that stayed with him his whole life.

Will did not let his shyness stop him from being a good salesperson. He didn't let hard times discourage him either. On one snowy sales trip, he rode a horse and sleigh. The sleigh fell over three times. All the brooms tumbled into the snow. Will picked them up. He dusted them off one by one. Then he lifted the sleigh and kept going. He sold all of his brooms that day.

Word spread about the hardworking Will Kellogg. In 1878, Will met a business owner named George King. He asked Will if he wanted a new job. Mr. King wanted Will to run his new broom factory in Dallas, Texas. Will knew he would miss his home. He also would miss his new girlfriend, Ella Davis. But Mr. King had offered him a good job. He decided to take it.

More than ten thousand people lived in Dallas, Texas, in the late 1800s.

Dallas was different from Battle Creek. It was much warmer. It was also bigger and dirtier. But Will's life was the same in one way. His days were filled with work, work, and more work.

Will seemed to be a natural business leader. But he did not like his job. Mr. King was not a good business owner. Will often had to fix the problems his boss had caused. He didn't like life in Dallas either. And he missed Ella.

Will returned home to Battle Creek in less than one year. He hoped he could make a good life for himself there.

2 WORK, WORK, AND MORE WORK

Will didn't have to look hard to find a new job. In 1880, he began working for his older brother, Dr. John Harvey Kellogg. John Harvey ran the Battle Creek Sanitarium. People called it the San. Many patients came to the San to be cured of illnesses. Other people came for healthy and restful vacations.

John Harvey Kellogg
was a respected doctor.

John Harvey took care of patients from all around the country and the world. Will took care of everything else. He kept track of how much money the San made. He ran errands. He kept up the building. And he made sure everything ran smoothly day after day.

The San's workers and patients called him W. K. They came to trust him and depend on him. "If you want anything done, go to W. K.," said one worker. "He will listen to your story and he will give you an answer and the answer will be perfectly fair."

Once again, W. K.'s life was filled with work, work, and more work. Still, he found time to marry Ella Davis on November 3, 1880. Their first child, Karl, was born the next year. John Leonard came in 1883. Their youngest child, Elizabeth Ann, was born in 1888.

W. K. loved his children. He wanted to be a good father. But his brother expected him to work many hours each day. Weeks went by when he hardly saw his sons and daughter. Many mornings, he left for work before they woke up. He often came home long after they had gone to bed.

W. K. married Ella Davis (LEFT) when he was twenty years old.

The
BATTLE CREEK SANITARIUM

VIEW OF MAIN BUILDING
Absolutely fire proof: 525 feet long: Six stories high: Largest and best-equipped health institution in the world: Branches in all parts of the world.

W. K. spent many long hours at the Battle Creek Sanitarium helping his brother run the business.

For all his hard work, W. K. earned very little money. John Harvey did not pay his brother much. W. K. struggled to buy the things his family needed.

Even though he was poor, W. K. wanted to help people the way his parents had. He gave money to friends and family members in need whenever he could. He let them stay in his home if they didn't have a place to live.

JOHN HARVEY KELLOGG'S FAMOUS CURES

W. K.'s brother had unusual ideas for curing his patients. His belief in a healthy diet and exercise was ahead of its time. He was also one of the first doctors to believe that smoking was bad for the body. But one of the most famous cures he believed in seems funny in modern times. It was known as the water cure. This cure called for many kinds of baths. Hot baths, cold baths, and steam baths were just some examples. Wrapping patients in cold, wet sheets (*right*) was another.

Nurses also sprayed patients with strong bursts of water. John Harvey believed that water helped to cleanse his patients of their illnesses.

W. K. also found ways to help poor patients at the San. He often talked his brother into letting them come to the San for free. Other times, W. K. paid for a patient himself.

W. K. liked helping sick people. But he did not always like his job. His brother bossed him around too much. And W. K. never seemed to earn enough money.

"I feel kind of blue," W. K. wrote in his diary. "[I] am afraid that I will always be a poor man." W. K. wondered if his life would ever change.

3 A FLAKY INVENTION

WK. not only kept the San running, but he also began to run many of his brother's other businesses. One of them was a health food company.

Dr. Kellogg believed in the importance of eating well. He did not let patients eat meat or fattening foods. He served them bland meals. The food had no salt, sugar, or spices.

Patients at the San felt better when they ate the doctor's food. Many of them wanted to keep eating it after they left. John Harvey's food company shipped packages of his health food to people's homes. Will was in charge of making sure all the packages were shipped on time.

Still, not all the San's patients liked the food. It was healthy. But it often did not taste very good. John Harvey asked W. K. to help him invent tastier health foods. Together they did experiments with new ingredients and cooking methods.

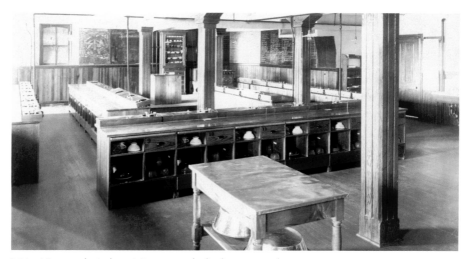

W. K. and John Harvey did their cooking experiments in the San's kitchen (ABOVE).

In 1894, the Kellogg brothers were working on a new health food recipe. First, they boiled wheat in water until it became a mushy dough. Then the brothers ran the dough through two smooth rollers. The rollers flattened the dough. The brothers scraped the dough off the rollers. Then they baked it. Later, they crumbled the baked dough and served it to patients. It was very healthy. But it tasted terrible.

One day, the brothers forgot about a batch of boiled wheat. They didn't remember it until two or three days later. They decided to run it through the rollers anyway.

W. K. scrapes the dough off the rollers to get little wheat flakes.

To their surprise, the dough came off the rollers in perfect little flakes. The brothers baked the flakes and tasted them. They were delicious! John Harvey wanted to crush the flakes into smaller pieces. But W. K. disagreed. He thought the patients would like the flakes whole. He was right. The wheat flakes were a big hit. The Kellogg brothers had invented a popular new food.

John Harvey and W. K. set up a new food company called Sanitas. Sanitas sold the wheat flakes. Thanks to W. K.'s hard work, sales grew and grew. Soon other local businesspeople caught on to the idea. They hoped to grow rich selling wheat flakes.

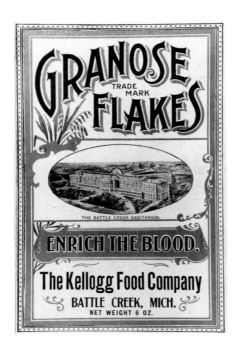

The Kellogg brothers called their wheat flakes Granose Flakes, as shown on this cereal box. The San is pictured in the center.

By 1904, about thirty other wheat flakes companies had opened in Battle Creek. These new companies took customers away from Sanitas. W. K. wanted to fight back. He had plans to put ads in magazines and newspapers. But John Harvey did not approve. He did not think it was right for a doctor to advertise his health food.

W. K. felt frustrated. But he had to do as his brother said. He decided to work on a new kind of cereal. He believed it would be a big seller. Best of all, other companies did not know how to make it. The cereal was cornflakes.

C. W. POST

In 1891, an ill businessman named Charles William Post (BELOW LEFT) came to stay at

the San. He liked what he saw. One year later, C. W. had opened his own sanitarium. At the same time, he also began to experiment with his own health foods. First, he invented a popular health drink called Postum. Then he created one of the first successful breakfast cereals. He called it Grape-Nuts. Post cereals are still popular around the world.

W. K. did many experiments. He wanted to make the cornflakes as tasty as they could be. One day, he added some sugar to the cornflake recipe. The flakes tasted great. But John Harvey was angry. He did not want sugar in any Sanitas foods.

W. K. grew more frustrated than ever. He was forty-five years old. He had run his brother's businesses for nearly twenty-five years. But John Harvey still bossed him around like a little brother.

W. K. quit working for his brother. He planned to start his own cornflake company. It would take a lot of hard work. But W. K. Kellogg had never been afraid of hard work.

4 KING OF CORN FLAKES

On February 19, 1906, W. K. opened the Battle Creek Toasted Corn Flake Company. That spring, he bought a run-down building. It became his company's first factory. He worked all day. Many nights, he couldn't sleep. Instead, he wrote down page after page of ideas for his company.

The first Kellogg cornflakes factory (ABOVE) was in Battle Creek, Michigan.

W. K. loved the challenge of running his own business. For him, beating other cereal companies was as much fun as any game. But he always tried to run his company honestly and fairly.

W. K. had big plans. He wanted to get millions of Americans to buy his cornflakes. To do that, he had to make sure his cereal tasted the best. He also needed to convince people that cereal was a good breakfast food.

People with health problems had been eating wheat flakes. But breakfast cereal was still a new idea to most Americans. Families often ate large meals in the morning. They might have meat, eggs, and pancakes or bread. Some of them even had pie for breakfast!

Farmers and families on the frontier used a lot of energy during the day. They needed a big breakfast. But by the 1900s, more and more people worked in factories or offices. They did not use as much energy at their jobs. A lighter breakfast seemed like a good idea. And Kellogg's Corn Flakes tasted better than most wheat flakes.

W. K. convinced people that cornflakes (BELOW) were a good breakfast food.

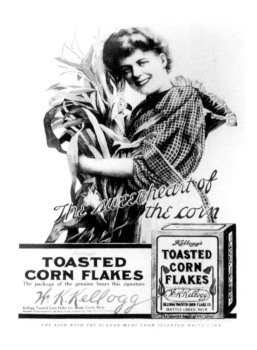

W. K. used his signature to set his cornflakes apart from other companies' flakes. This is one of his advertisements from 1906.

Soon other companies began to make cornflakes. They had names such as Korn-Kinks, Lucky Boy Corn Flakes, and Corn-O-Plenty. W. K. labeled all of his cereal boxes with his signature in red ink. That way, no one would mistake a competitor's corn flakes for his.

W. K.'s business was a great success. But in the summer of 1907, a fire burned down his factory. W. K. had never let a problem discourage him before. He did not give up after the fire either. Instead, he decided to build a brand-new factory. He would fill this factory with modern machines. They would make more cereal than ever.

The new factory was up and running six months after the fire. New machines allowed workers to make more than four thousand cases of cereal each day. W. K. sold them all.

W. K. did not save up most of the money his company earned. Instead, he spent it to win over more customers. He hired salespeople to bring free samples of his cornflakes to people's homes. He shipped free cornflakes to grocers. They handed them out to shoppers. His company also gave away prizes to children who bought his cereal. One of the first prizes was a jungle picture book.

W. K.'s boxes of cornflakes (RIGHT) sometimes held prizes.

W. K. also spent more money on advertisements than most other cereal makers. He put his ads on streetcars, in newspapers, and in magazines. He paid for signs in big cities. His company also put on radio shows. These shows entertained people. They also told listeners about W. K.'s cereal.

This advertisement for Kellogg's Corn Flakes came out in 1908.

Good Taste in Business

W. K. hired people to help him invent new cereals. He tested each one. Then he decided if he liked it. If he didn't, he wouldn't sell it. He had a knack for knowing what people would buy. One day, some workers came to him with a new cereal made from rice.

W. K. poured some milk on it and took a bite. "That will be a successful product," he said. And he was right. The cereal was Rice Krispies.

W. K.'s many plans and ads paid off. His company grew. He became rich. He began to wear nicer clothing. He moved to a new house. He even bought a new invention, an automobile. But not everything was going well for W. K. All of his money could not keep his wife, Ella, healthy.

W. K., shown here at age sixty-three, made his company strong by working hard.

Over the years, Ella seemed to have one illness after another. W. K. paid for the best doctors and cures. None of it worked. In 1912, Ella died at the age of fifty-four.

W. K. missed Ella terribly. To forget his loneliness, he spent more time than ever at his work. His company grew stronger and stronger. Meanwhile, other cereal companies shut down.

W. K. began to make other cereals. They, too, became popular. He opened factories and offices across the United States. In 1914, he opened his first factory outside the United States. He built it in Canada. The Kellogg name had become famous. And W. K. was known as the King of Corn Flakes.

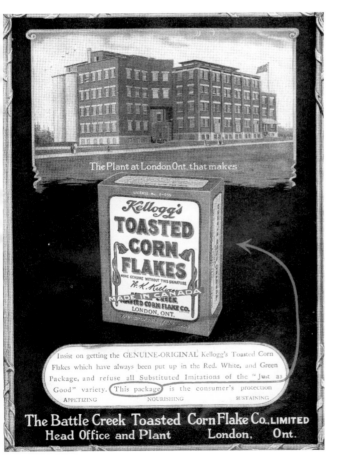

This advertisement shows W. K.'s plant in London, Ontario, Canada.

5 HELPING PEOPLE HELP THEMSELVES

On New Year's Day in 1918, W. K. made a big change in his life. He married a quiet, hardworking woman. Her name was Carrie Staines. Carrie was a doctor at the Battle Creek Sanitarium. W. K. respected the work she did there.

W. K. and Carrie lived a good life together. At the age of fifty-eight, W. K. had become a very rich man. He and Carrie took many vacations. Sometimes they rode across the country in a large automobile. W. K. called it the Ark. The Ark had room for beds, a kitchen, a shower, and a bathroom. That was unheard of in the early 1920s.

W. K. (CENTER) stands in front of the Ark in Battle Creek before leaving to tour all the U.S. state capitals.

The Kelloggs traveled by ship to faraway places. They went to Hawaii, Australia, Egypt, and other parts of the world. On these travels, W. K. forgot about work. He relaxed and caught up on sleep. And he ate lots of chocolate candy bars and drank chocolate sodas. These were his favorite treats.

W. K. also bought huge homes in Michigan, California, and Florida. He traveled between them during the year. Best of all, he made a childhood dream come true. He bought a ranch in Southern California. Then he filled it with beautiful Arabian horses.

W. K. built this home on Gull Lake in Michigan.

W. K. (STANDING) and his son John L. Kellogg at W.K.'s Arabian horse ranch

W. K. enjoyed being able to spend money on his adventures. But he never stopped helping others. He still gave money to his friends, family, and workers in need. He cared for his workers in other ways too. In the 1920s, W. K. opened a free day care center in his main factory in Battle Creek. The center paid for free medical and dental exams to keep the children healthy.

W. K. liked helping the children of his hometown. He paid for a new youth recreation center with a swimming pool. He helped pay for a new elementary school. He named it the Ann J. Kellogg School, after his mother. He also opened a new junior high school and community auditorium.

The Ann J. Kellogg School in Battle Creek, Michigan

W. K. wanted to give many more people the chance to make their lives better. In 1930, he opened the W. K. Kellogg Foundation. A foundation is an organization that gives away money to help people and communities. W. K. chose leaders he trusted to run the foundation. He said, "We will help people to help themselves." That first year, the foundation gave away $26,000 of W. K.'s money.

W. K. AND THE GREAT DEPRESSION

The Great Depression of the 1930s was a difficult time in American history. Many companies closed. Millions of men and women lost their jobs. W. K. found ways to help. He created more jobs at his factory. He also paid for a new park to be built on his factory's land. That meant hiring many workers. The workers cleared the land for gardens. They also built a playground, a pool, and tennis courts.

W. K. with his German shepherd standing in front of the W. K. Kellogg Foundation in Battle Creek.

At first, the foundation gave all of its money to small communities in Michigan. It helped pay for new schools, libraries, hospitals, and health clinics. This work became known as the Michigan Community Health Project.

By the 1940s, W. K.'s foundation began to help people in other parts of the country. It also helped communities in Latin America and Europe. Over time, it began giving to communities all around the world. The foundation's money has helped in many ways. It has been used to make health care better. It has given people a chance to get a good education. And it has helped communities end poverty in poorer countries.

W. K.'s foundation helps people around the world. He was seventy-nine when this photo was taken.

W. K.'s generosity made him more famous than ever. But he did not like all the attention. In his old age, he tried his best to lead a quiet, private life. He died on October 6, 1951. He was ninety-one years old.

W. K. Kellogg's hard work lives on. The Kellogg Company sells its cereal to people all around the world. And the W. K. Kellogg Foundation continues to help people help themselves.

TIMELINE

In the year . . .

1878   W. K. moved to Dallas, Texas, to run a new   Age 18
        broom factory.

1879   he returned to Battle Creek, Michigan.

1880   he began working for his brother John
        Harvey at the Battle Creek Sanitarium.
        W. K. married Ella Davis on November 3.

1894   he and his brother invented the wheat flake.   Age 34

1906   he opened the Battle Creek Toasted Corn
        Flake Company on February 19, 1906.

1907   his company's first factory burned down on
        the Fourth of July.

1912   he paid for the largest advertising sign in   Age 52
        the world, in New York City.
        his first wife, Ella, died.
        his company began putting out other cereals.

1914   he opened his first foreign factory.

1918   he married Dr. Carrie Staines on January 1.   Age 57

1922   he officially renamed his company the
        Kellogg Company.

1925   he bought an Arabian horse ranch.
        he gave the city of Battle Creek many gifts
        in honor of his sixty-fifth birthday.

1929   the Great Depression began.

1930   W. K. started the W. K. Kellogg Foundation.   Age 70

1942   the Great Depression ended.

1951   W. K. Kellogg died on October 6.   Age 91

2005   the W. K. Kellogg Foundation celebrated its
        seventy-fifth birthday.

2006   the Kellogg Company celebrated its one
        hundredth birthday.

CEREAL, CEREAL, CEREAL

Americans eat a lot of cereal. They buy around 2.7 billion boxes of it each year. Laid end to end, that many cereal boxes would reach from Earth to the Moon and back! W. K. Kellogg's company has invented many cereals over the years. So have other companies such as Post, General Mills, and Quaker Oats. Here are some popular cereals and when they were first sold. How many of them have you eaten?

1897 – Post's Grape-Nuts
1906 – Kellogg's Corn Flakes
1924 – General Mills's Wheaties
1928 – Kellogg's Rice Krispies
1941 – General Mills's Cheerios (first called Cheerioates)
1942 – Kellogg's Raisin Bran
1952 – Kellogg's Frosted Flakes
1956 – Kellogg's Special K
1957 – Post's Alpha Bits
1959 – Kellogg's Corn Pops (first called Sugar Pops)
1961 – General Mills's Total
1963 – Kellogg's Fruit Loops
1964 – General Mills's
          Lucky Charms
1965 – Kellogg's Apple Jacks

Special K and Rice Krispies are just two of the cereals that Kellogg's still makes.

FURTHER READING

Epstein, Rachel. *W. K. Kellogg: Generous Genius.* **New York: Children's Press, 2000.** Epstein tells the story of W. K. Kellogg.

Gould, William. *VGM Business Portraits: Kellogg's.* **Lincolnwood, IL: VGM Career Horizons, 1997.** This book explores the business that W. K. Kellogg created.

Kellogg Kitchens. *The Kellogg's Cookbook: 200 Classic Recipes for Today's Kitchen.* **Edited by Judith Choate. New York: Bulfinch Press, 2006.** This cookbook is packed full of recipes and photographs from Kellogg's.

Mierau, Christina. *Accept No Substitutes: The History of American Advertising.* **Minneapolis: Lerner Publishing Company, 2000.** Mierau tells about the history of advertising—and how business owners just like W. K. Kellogg used it to sell their products.

Peterson, Tiffany. *W. K. Kellogg.* **Portsmouth, NH: Heinemann, 2003**. This title provides the life story of W. K. Kellogg at a slightly lower reading level.

Ruth, Amy. *Growing Up in the Great Depression 1929 to 1941.* **Minneapolis: Lerner Publishing Company, 2003.** This book describes life for children who lived through the Great Depression.

WEBSITES

American Cereal Council: Fun Facts
http://www.americancerealcouncil.org/facts_trivia.htm
Learn some wacky facts about cereal on this Web page.

Kellogg's.com
http://www.kelloggs.com/us This is the official website of
W. K. Kellogg's company.

Kellogg's Company History
http://www.kellogg100.com/history.html This interactive
website tells about the history of W. K. Kellogg and his
company.

SELECT BIBLIOGRAPHY

Bruce, Scott, and Bill Crawford. *Cerealizing America: The
Unsweetened Story of American Breakfast Cereal.* Boston:
Faber and Faber, 1995.

Powell, Horace B. *The Original Has This Signature—W. K.
Kellogg.* Englewood Cliffs, NJ: Prentice Hall, Inc., 1956.

W. K. Kellogg Foundation
http://www.wkkf.org

W. K. Kellogg Foundation. *W. K. Kellogg Foundation: The
First Half-Century, 1930–1980.* Battle Creek, MI: W. K.
Kellogg Foundation, 1979.

INDEX

Arabian horses, 8, 38, 39

Battle Creek, 6, 12, 13, 24, 39
Battle Creek Sanitarium (the San), 14, 15, 19, 20, 21, 36
Battle Creek Toasted Corn Flake Company, 27, 28

Canada, 35
cornflakes, 24–25, 28, 29, 30, 31, 32, 35

Dallas, Texas, 12
Davis, Ella. *See* Kellogg, Ella Davis

Kellogg, Ann (mother), 9, 40
Kellogg, Elizabeth Ann (daughter), 16
Kellogg, Ella Davis (wife), 12, 13, 16, 33–34

Kellogg, John (father), 9
Kellogg, John Harvey (brother) , 5, 14, 15, 17, 18, 20, 21, 23, 24, 25, 26
Kellogg, John Leonard (son), 16, 39
Kellogg, Karl (son), 16
Kellogg, W. K., Foundation, 5, 41–42, 43
King, George, 12, 13
King of Corn Flakes, 35

Post, Charles William, 25

Sanitas, 23, 24, 25
Seventh-day Adventists, 9
Staines, Carrie, 36, 37

Acknowledgments

For photographs and artwork: © Bettmann/CORBIS, pp. 4, 37, 39; © William Henry Fox Talbot/Hulton Archive/Getty Images, p. 7; © age fotostock/SuperStock, p. 8; Courtesy of Kellogg Company Archives, pp. 10, 15, 16, 17, 22, 24, 28, 31, 32, 33, 34, 35, 38, 40, 42, 43; Library of Congress, pp. 11 (LC-USZC4-2365), 25 (LC-USZ62-121002); Lamar and Commerce Streets, Dallas, c.1890 (b/w photo) by American Photographer, (19th century) © Dallas Historical Society, Texas/Bridgeman Art Library, p. 12; Image supplied by lifestylelaboratory.com, pp. 18, 21; AP/Wide World Photos, pp. 23, 45; © photocuisine/Corbis, p. 29; © Frederic Lewis/Getty Images, p. 30.
Cover: Courtesy of Kellogg Company Archives.
Back cover: Courtesy of Kellogg Company Archives.

For quoted material: pp. 15, 19, 33, 41, Horace B. Powell, *The Original Has this Signature—W. K. Kellogg* (Englewood Cliffs, NJ: Prentice Hall, Inc., 1956).